Good Hunting

First published 1907 by Harper & Brothers Publishers
Special Contents Copyright © 2000 by Palladium Press
First Skyhorse Publishing edition 2014

Skyhorse Publishing books may be purchased in bulk at special discounts for sales promotion, corporate gifts, fund-raising, or educational purposes. Special editions can also be created to specifications. For details, contact the Special Sales Department, Skyhorse Publishing, 307 West 36th Street, 11th Floor, New York, NY 10018 or info@skyhorsepublishing.com.

Skyhorse® and Skyhorse Publishing® are registered trademarks of Skyhorse Publishing, Inc.®, a Delaware corporation.

Visit our website at www.skyhorsepublishing.com.

10 9 8 7

Library of Congress Cataloging-in-Publication Data is available on file.

Cover design by Victoria Bellavia
Cover photo from the public domain

ISBN: 978-1-62873-797-4
Ebook ISBN: 978-1-62914-052-0

Printed in China

A WOUNDED BULL ELK

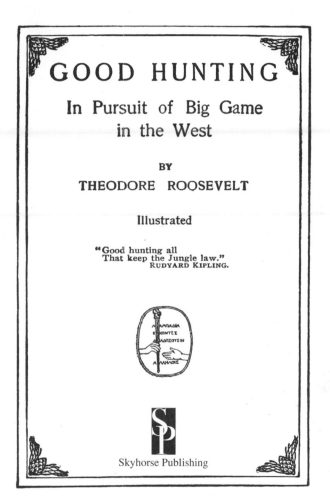

GOOD HUNTING

In Pursuit of Big Game in the West

BY

THEODORE ROOSEVELT

Illustrated

"Good hunting all
That keep the Jungle law."
RUDYARD KIPLING.

Skyhorse Publishing

Publisher's Note

THIS book offers to younger readers a
series of pictures of out-door life and big-
game hunting in the West. More than
this, the author makes us feel not only
the zest of sport and adventure, but also
the interest attaching to the habits and
peculiarities of the remarkable animals
which he describes. It is a field-book,
since it is written by a true sportsman out
of his own experiences, and its general
spirit tends to a better appreciation of the
value of close observation of animal life.
The elk, bear, goats, deer, and other
animals which are described, represent
the most remarkable large fauna of our
country. These descriptions, by one

Publisher's Note

whose acquaintance with them has been so intimate, have an added value in view of the diminution in their number.

It is interesting, also, to remember that the influence of the author has been constantly exerted in favor of the preservation of big game and the maintenance of national parks and forest reserves, which, in addition to other advantages, include the protection of these noble forms of animal life.

This series of articles upon big-game hunting was written for *Harper's Round Table*, and published therein in 1897. The picture of ranch-life which forms the closing chapter appeared in *Harper's Round Table* in 1896. These articles are now presented together in book form for the first time after consultation with the author. For the title of the book and the proof-reading the publishers are responsible.

Contents

Illustrations

The Wapiti,
or Round-horned Elk

I

THE WAPITI, OR ROUND-HORNED ELK

 NO country of the temperate zone can begin to compare with South Asia, and, above all, tropical and subtropical Africa, in the number and size of those great beasts of the chase which are known to hunters as big game; but after the Indian and African hunting-grounds, the best are still those of North America. Until a few years before 1897 there were large regions, even in the United States, where the teeming myriads of wild game, though of far fewer and less varied

13

Good Hunting

species, almost equalled the multitudes found in South Africa, and much surpassed those found anywhere else in point of numbers, though inferior in variety to those of India.

This, however, is now a thing of the past. The bison, which was the most characteristic animal of the American fauna, has been practically exterminated. There remained in 1897, however, a fair abundance of all other kinds of game. Perhaps, on the whole, the one affording most sport from the stand-point of the hardy and skilful hunter is the big-horn, though in size and in magnificence of horn it is surpassed by some of the wild sheep of Asia.

There is a spice of danger in the pursuit of the grizzly-bear—the largest of all the land bears—especially in Alaska, where it is even larger than its Kamtchatkan brother. The moose and the wapiti—

14

The Wapiti, or Round-horned Elk

ordinarily called the elk—are closely re-
lated to the Old-World representatives of
their kind; but the moose is a little larger
and the wapiti very much larger than
any of their European or Asiatic kinsfolk. In particular, the elk, or wapiti,
is the stateliest of all deer, and the most
beautiful of American game beasts.

It is a pity we cannot always call the
wapiti by its right name, but the hunters
and settlers never know him as anything
but the elk, and I fear it would be
pedantry to try to establish his rightful
title. In former days the elk ranged to
tide-water on the Atlantic coast. A few
lingered in Pennsylvania until 1869, and
throughout the middle of the century,
they were abundant on the great plains.
In 1888 I shot one on the Little Missouri,
however. In many parts of the Rocky
Mountains and of the Coast Range the
species is still as abundant as ever, and

15

this is especially true of northwestern Wyoming, since that great animal-preserve the Yellowstone Park swarms with elk, and is their natural nursery and breeding-ground.

The elk is the lordliest of his kind throughout the world. The Scotch stag is a pygmy but a fourth his size. The stags of eastern Europe are larger than those of Scotland, and in Asia larger still, approaching in size a small wapiti. They are all substantially alike except in size.

The wapiti is rather easier to kill than the deer, because his size makes it easier to see him; and he is slower in his movements, so that he is easier to hit. When pressed he can gallop very hard for a few hundred yards, but soon becomes tired. The trot is his natural gait, and this he can keep up for hours at a time, going at a pace which makes it necessary for a horse to gallop smartly to overtake him,

The Wapiti, or Round-horned Elk

and clearing great logs in his stride, while he dodges among the thick timber in a really marvellous way, when one comes to think of the difficulty he must have in handling his great antlers.

Late in September the rut begins, and then the elk gather in huge bands, while the great bulls fight vicious battles for leadership. Hunters call this the whistling-time, because throughout its continuance the bulls are very noisy, continually challenging one another. Their note is really not much like a whistle. It consists of two or three bars, rising and then falling, ending with a succession of grunts; the tone of voice varies greatly in different individuals; but when heard at a little distance in the heart of the great wooded wilderness the sound is very musical, and to me—and, I suppose, to most hunters—it is one of the most attractive sounds in all nature.

17

Good Hunting

At this season the big bulls are quite easy to approach by any man at all skilled in still-hunting, for their incessant challenging betrays their whereabouts, and they are so angry and excited as to be less watchful than usual. Some of my most pleasurable memories of hunting are connected with stalking some great bull-elk in frosty weather, when the woods rang with his challenges.

One evening in early October I was camped high among the mountains of western Montana. We were travelling with a pack-train, and had pitched our small tent among some firs by a brook, while the horses grazed in the little park or meadow close by. Elk were plentiful round about. We had seen their trails everywhere, and late in the afternoon we had caught a glimpse of a band of cows as they disappeared among the pines.

The Wapiti, or Round-horned Elk

Towards morning I was awakened by hearing a bull challenge not very far from camp. The sound of the challenge kept coming nearer and nearer, and finally I heard one of the horses snort loudly in response, evidently the elk saw them, and, not making out exactly what they were, was coming down to join them. Sometimes horses will stampede when thus approached; but our ponies were veterans, and were very tired, and evidently had no intention of leaving their good pasture.

Sitting up in my blankets, I could tell from the sound that they were still in the park, and then the challenge of the bull came pealing up not three hundred yards from the tent. This was more than I could stand, and I jumped up and put on my shoes and jacket. The moon was bright, but shooting by moonlight is very deceptive, and I doubt whether I would

19

Good Hunting

have hit him even had I got down to the park in time. However, he had moved on before I got down, and I heard his challenge in the woods beyond.

Looking at my watch, I saw that it was nearly dawn. I returned to the tent and laid down as I was under the blankets, and shivered and dozed for half an hour, then I came back to the meadow, where the pack - ponies stood motionless. In the brightening light the moon paled, and I was very soon able to pick out the bull's trail on the frost-covered ground, where it was almost as plain as if he had been walking in snow. I saw that he had struck up a long valley, from which a pass led into a wooded basin. At the top of the pass I lost the trail entirely, and as it was almost impossible to see for any distance through the woods, I came to the conclusion that the best thing to do was to sit down and await events.

20

The Wapiti, or Round-horned Elk

I did not have long to wait. In a
couple of minutes the bugle of a bull came
echoing across the basin through the
frosty morning. Evidently my friend
was still travelling, hunting for some
possibly weaker rival. Almost immediately I heard far off another answering
the challenge, and I stood up and medi-
tated what to do. There was very little
air, but such as there was blew to one
side of the spot from which the last challenge seemed to come, and I immediately
struck off at a trot through the woods to
get below the wind.

The answer to the challenge had evidently greatly excited the bull whose
trail I had been following; he called every
two or three minutes. The other answer
was somewhat more irregular, and as I
drew nearer I could tell from the volume
of sound that the second challenge was
from some big master-bull, who probably

21

Good Hunting

had his herd around him, and was roaring defiance at his would-be despoiler, for the single bull was doubtless on the lookout for some weaker one whom he could supplant as master of a herd.

It was likely that the second bull, being a herd-master, would have the larger antlers, and I therefore preferred to get a shot at him. However, I was doomed to disappointment. As I groped towards the herd, and was within a couple of hundred yards, as I knew by the volume of sound, I almost stumbled upon a small spike-bull, who was evidently loitering about the outskirts of the herd, not daring to go too near the bad-tempered old chief. This little bull dashed away, giving the alarm, and a clash in the bushes soon told that the herd was following him.

But luck favored me. The master-bull, being absorbed in thoughts of his rival, evidently suspected that the cows

The Wapiti, or Round-horned Elk

had some thought of fleeing from him, and, as they ran, tried to hold them together. I ran too, going at full speed, with the hope of cutting him off; in this I failed, but I came almost face to face with the very bull which I had been following from camp, and which had evidently followed the herd at full speed as soon as they ran.

Great was his astonishment when he saw me. He pulled up so suddenly to wheel round that he almost fell on his side; then off he went in a plunging gallop of terror; but he was near by, and stepping to one side I covered an opening between two trees, firing the minute he appeared. A convulsive leap showed that the bullet had struck, and after him I went at full speed. In a short time I saw him again, walking along with drooping head, and again I fired into his flank; he seemed to pay no attention to the shot,

Good Hunting

but walked forward a few steps, then halted, faltered, and fell on his side. In another second I had placed my rifle against a tree, and was admiring his shapely form and massive antlers.

A Cattle-killing Bear

II

A CATTLE-KILLING BEAR

THERE were, in 1897, a few grizzlies left here and there along the Little Missouri, usually in large bottoms covered with an almost impenetrable jungle of timber and thorny brush. In the old days they used to be very plentiful in this region, and ventured boldly out on the prairie. The Little Missouri region was a famous hunting-ground for both the white trappers and the Indian hunters in those old days when the far West was still a wilderness, and the men who trapped beaver would

Good Hunting

wander for years over the plains and mountains and see no white faces save those of their companions.

Indeed, at that time the Little Missouri was very dangerous country, as it was the debatable-ground between many powerful Indian tribes, and was only visited by formidable war-parties and hunting-parties. In consequence of nobody daring to live there, game swarmed—buffalo, elk, deer, antelope, mountain-sheep, and bear. The bears were then very bold, and the hunters had little difficulty in getting up to them, for they were quite as apt to attack as to run away.

But when, in 1880, the Northern Pacific Railroad reached the neighborhood of the Little Missouri, all this changed forever. The game that for untold ages had trodden out their paths over the prairies and along the river-bottoms vanished, as the Indians that had hunted it also vanished.

A Cattle-killing Bear

The bold white hunters also passed away
with the bears they had chased and the
red foes against whom they had warred.
In their places the ranchman came in with
great herds of cattle and horses and
flocks of sheep, and built their log cabins
and tilled their scanty garden-patches,
and cut down the wild hay for winter
fodder. Now bears are as shy as they
are scarce. No grizzly in such a settled
region would dream of attacking a man
unprovoked, and they pass their days in
the deepest thickets, so that it is almost
impossible to get at them. I never
killed a bear in the neighborhood of my
former ranch, though I have shot quite a
number some hundreds of miles to the
west in the Rocky Mountains.

Usually the bears live almost ex-
clusively on roots, berries, insects, and
the like. In fact, there is always something grotesque and incongruous in com-

Good Hunting

paring the bear's vast size, and his formidable claws and teeth, with the uses to which those claws and teeth are normally put. At the end of the season the claws, which are very long in spring, sometimes become so much blunted as to be tender, because the bear has worked on hard ground digging roots and the like.

Bears often graze on the fresh tender spring grass. Berries form their especial delight, and they eat them so greedily when in season as to become inordinately fat. Indeed, a bear in a berry - patch frequently grows so absorbed in his work as to lose his wariness, and as he makes a good deal of noise himself in breaking branches and gobbling down the fruit, he is exposed to much danger from the hunter.

Besides roots and berries, the bear will feed on any small living thing he en-

A Cattle-killing Bear

counters. If in plundering a squirrel's *cache* he comes upon some young squirrels, down they go in company with the hoarded nuts. He is continually knocking to pieces and overturning old dead logs for the sake of devouring the insects living beneath them. If, when such a log is overturned, mice, shrews, or chipmunks are found underneath, the bear promptly scoops them into his mouth while they are still dazed by the sudden inrush of light. All this seems rather ludicrous as the life work of an animal of such huge proportions and such vast strength.

Sometimes, however, a bear will take to killing fresh meat for itself. Indeed, I think it is only its clumsiness that prevents it from becoming an habitual flesh-eater. Deer are so agile that bears can rarely get them; yet on occasions not only deer, but moose, buffalo, and elk fall victims to them. Wild game,

Good Hunting

however, are so shy, so agile, and so alert that it is only rarely they afford meals to old Ephraim—as the mountain hunters call the grizzly.

Domestic animals are slower, more timid, more clumsy, and with far duller senses. It is on these that the bear by preference preys when he needs fresh meat. I have never, myself, known one to kill horses; but I have been informed that the feat is sometimes performed, usually in spring; and the ranchman who told me insisted that when a bear made his rush he went with such astonishing speed that the horse was usually overtaken before it got well under way.

The favorite food of a bear, however, if he really wants fresh meat, is a hog or sheep—by preference the former. If a bear once gets into the habit of visiting a sheepfold or pigpen, it requires no slight skill and watchfulness to keep

A Cattle-killing Bear

him out. As for swine, they dread bears more than anything else. A drove of half-wild swine will make head against a wolf or panther; but the bear scatters them in a panic. This feat is entirely justifiable, for a bear has a peculiar knack in knocking down a hog, and then literally eating him alive, in spite of his fearful squealing.

Every now and then bears take to killing cattle regularly. Sometimes the criminal is a female with cubs; sometimes an old male in spring, when he is lean, and has the flesh hunger upon him. But on one occasion a very large and cunning bear, some twenty-five miles below my ranch, took to cattle-killing early in the summer, and continued it through the fall. He made his home in a very densely wooded bottom; but he wandered far and wide, and I have myself frequently seen his great, half-human footprints

Good Hunting

leading along some narrow divide, or across some great plateau, where there was no cover whatever, and where he must have gone at night. During the daytime, when on one of these expeditions, he would lie up in some timber *coulée*, and return to the river-bottoms after dark, so that no one ever saw him; but his tracks were seen very frequently.

He began operations on the bottom where he had his den. He at first took to lying in wait for the cattle as they came down to drink, when he would seize some animal, usually a fat young steer or heifer, knocking it over by sheer force. In his furious rush he sometimes broke the back with a terrific blow from his fore-paw; at other times he threw the animal over and bit it to death. The rest of the herd never made any effort to retaliate, but fled in terror. Very soon

34

A Cattle-killing Bear

the cattle would not go down on this bottom at all; then he began to wander over the adjoining bottoms, and finally to make excursions far off in the broken country. Evidently he would sometimes at night steal along a *coulée* until he found cattle lying down on the hillside, and then approach cautiously and seize his prey.

Usually the animals he killed were cows or steers; and noticing this, a certain ranchman in the neighborhood used to boast that a favorite bull on his ranch, of which he was particularly proud, would surely account for the bear if the latter dared to attack him. The boast poved vain. One day a cow-boy riding down a lonely *coulée* came upon the scene of what had evidently been a very hard conflict. There were deep marks of hoofs and claws in the soft soil, bushes were smashed down where the struggling

35

Good Hunting

combatants had pressed against and over them, and a little farther on lay the remains of the bull.

He must have been seized by surprise; probably the great bear rushed at him from behind, or at one side, and fastened upon him so that he had no fair chance to use his horns. Nevertheless, he made a gallant struggle for his life, staggering to and fro trying to shake off his murderous antagonist, and endeavoring in vain to strike back over his shoulder; but all was useless. Even his strength could not avail against the might of his foe, and the cruel claws and teeth tore out his life. At last the gallant bull fell and breathed his last, and the bear feasted on the carcass.

The angry ranchman swore vengeance, and set a trap for the bear, hoping it would return. The sly old beast, however, doubtless was aware that the body had

A Cattle-killing Bear

been visited, for he never came back, but returned to the river-bottom, and again from time to time was heard of as slaying some animal. However, at last his fate overtook him. Early one morning a cow was discovered just killed and not yet eaten, the bear having probably been scared off. Immediately the ranchman put poison in the bait which the bear had thus himself left, and twenty-four hours later the shaggy beast was found lying dead within a dozen yards of his last victim.

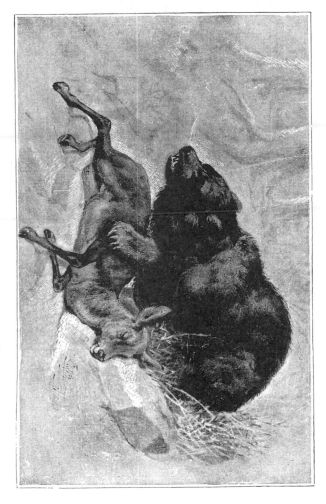

THE GRIZZLY AND A VICTIM

A Christmas Buck

III

A CHRISTMAS BUCK

HROUGHOUT most of the ranch country there are two kinds of deer, the black-tail and the white-tail. The white-tail is the same as the deer of the East; it is a beautiful creature, a marvel of lightness and grace in all its movements, and it loves to dwell in thick timber, so that in the plains country it is almost confined to the heavily wooded river bottoms. The black-tail is somewhat larger, with a different and very peculiar gait, con-sisting of a succession of stiff-legged

Good Hunting

bounds, all four feet striking the earth at the same time. Its habits are likewise very different, as it is a bolder animal and much fonder of the open country. Among the Rockies it is found in the deep forests, but it prefers scantily wooded regions, and in the plains country it dwells by choice in the rough hills, spending the day in the patches of ash or cedar among the ravines. In 1882 the black-tail was very much more abundant than the white-tail almost everywhere in the West, but owing to the nature of its haunts it is more easily killed out, and in 1897, though both species had decreased in numbers, the white-tail was on the whole the more common.

My ranch-house was situated on a heavily wooded bottom, one of the places where the white-tail were found. On one occasion I killed one from the ranch veranda, and two or three times I shot

A Christmas Buck

them within half a mile of the house. Nevertheless, they are so cunning and stealthy in their ways, and the cover is so dense, that usually, although one may know of their existence right in one's neighborhood, there is more chance of getting game by going off eight or ten miles into the broken country of the black-tail.

One Christmas I was to be at the ranch, and I made up my mind that I would try to get a good buck for our Christmas dinner; for I had not had much time to hunt that fall, and Christmas was almost upon us before we started to lay in our stock of winter meat. So I arranged with one of the cow-boys to make an all-day's hunt through some rugged hills on the other side of the river, where we knew there were black-tail.

We were up soon after three o'clock, when it was yet as dark as at midnight.

43

Good Hunting

We had a long day's work before us, and so we ate a substantial breakfast, then put on our fur caps, coats, and mittens, and walked out into the cold night. The air was still, but it was biting weather, and we pulled our caps down over our ears as we walked towards the rough, low stable where the two hunting-ponies had been put overnight. In a few minutes we were jogging along on our journey.

There was a powder of snow over the ground, and this and the brilliant star-light enabled us to see our way without difficulty. The river was frozen hard, and the hoofs of the horses rang on the ice as they crossed. For a while we followed the wagon road, and then struck off into a cattle trail which led up into a long *coulée*. After a while this faded out, and we began to work our way along the divide, not without caution, for in broken

44

A Christmas Buck

countries it is hard to take a horse during darkness. Indeed, we found we had left a little too early, for there was hardly a glimmer of dawn when we reached our proposed hunting-grounds. We left the horses in a sheltered nook where there was abundance of grass, and strode off on foot, numb after the ride.

The dawn brightened rapidly, and there was almost light enough for shooting when we reached a spur overlooking a large basin around whose edges there were several wooded *coulées*. Here we sat down to wait and watch. We did not have to wait long, for just as the sun was coming up on our right hand we caught a glimpse of something moving at the mouth of one of the little ravines some hundreds of yards distant. Another glance showed us that it was a deer feeding, while another behind it was walking leisurely in our direction.

Good Hunting

There was no time to be lost, and, sliding back over the crest, we trotted off around a spur until we were in line with the quarry, and then walked rapidly towards them. Our only fear was lest they should move into some position where they would see us; and this fear was justified. While still one hundred yards from the mouth of the *coulée* in which we had seen the feeding deer, the second one, which all the time had been walking slowly in our direction, came out on a ridge crest to one side of our course. It saw us at once and halted short; it was only a spike buck, but there was no time to lose, for we needed meat, and in another moment it would have gone off, giving the alarm to its companion. So I dropped on one knee, and fired just as it turned.

From the jump it gave I was sure it was hit, but it disappeared over the hill, and at the same time the big buck, its

46

A Christmas Buck

companion, dashed out of the *coulée* in front, across the basin. It was broadside to me, and not more than one hundred yards distant; but a running deer is difficult to hit, and though I took two shots, both missed, and it disappeared behind another spur.

This looked pretty bad, and I felt rather blue as I climbed up to look at the trail of the spike. I was cheered to find blood, and as there was a good deal of snow here and there it was easy to follow it; nor was it long before we saw the buck moving forward slowly, evidently very sick. We did not disturb him, but watched him until he turned down into a short ravine a quarter of a mile off; he did not come out, and we sat down and waited nearly an hour to give him time to get stiff. When we reached the valley, one went down each side so as to be sure to get him when he jumped up. Our

Good Hunting

caution was needless, however, for we failed to start him; and on hunting through some of the patches of brush we found him stretched out already dead.

This was satisfactory; but still it was not the big buck, and we started out again after dressing and hanging up the deer. For many hours we saw nothing, and we had swung around within a couple of miles of the horses before we sat down behind a screen of stunted cedars for a last look. After attentively scanning every patch of brush in sight, we were about to go on when the attention of both of us was caught at the same moment by seeing a big buck deliberately get up, turn round, and then lie down again in a grove of small, leafless trees lying opposite to us on a hill-side with a southern exposure. He had evidently very nearly finished his day's rest, but was not quite ready to go

48

A Christmas Buck

out to feed; and his restlessness cost him his life.

As we now knew just where he was, the work was easy. We marked a place on the hill-top a little above and to one side of him; and while the cow-boy remained to watch him, I drew back and walked leisurely round to where I could get a shot. When nearly up to the crest I crawled into view of the patch of brush, rested my elbows on the ground, and gently tapped two stones together. The buck rose nimbly to his feet, and at seventy yards afforded me a standing shot, which I could not fail to turn to good account.

A winter day is short, and twilight had come before we had packed both bucks on the horses; but with our game behind our saddles we did not feel either fatigue, or hunger or cold, while the horses trotted steadily homeward. The moon was a

49

Good Hunting

few days old, and it gave us light until we reached the top of the bluffs by the river and saw across the frozen stream the gleam from the fire-lit windows of the ranch-house.

The Timber-wolf

IV

THE TIMBER-WOLF

THERE are two kinds of wolves found in the United States. One is the little coyote or prairie-wolf, or barking-wolf, which never was found in the Eastern States, being an animal of the open country; the other is the big wolf, sometimes called the buffalo-wolf, and sometimes the timber-wolf or gray wolf, which was formerly found everywhere from the Atlantic to the Pacific. In some districts it runs to color varieties of different kinds—red, black, or white.

53

Good Hunting

The coyote is not at all a formidable beast, and holds its own quite persistently until civilization is well advanced in a country. Coyotes are not dangerous to either man or the larger domestic animals. Lambs, young pigs, hens, and cats often become their prey, and if very hungry several of them will combine to attack a young calf. In consequence, farmers and ranchers kill them whenever the chance offers; but they do not do damage which is even appreciable when compared with the ravages of their grim big brother, the gray wolf, which in many sections of the West is a veritable scourge of the stock-men.

The big wolves shrink back before the growth of the thickly settled districts, and in the Eastern States they often tend to disappear even from districts that are uninhabited, save by a few wilderness hunters. They have thus disappeared

54

The Timber-wolf

almost entirely from Maine, the Adirondacks, and the Alleghanies, although here and there they are said to be returning to their old haunts.

Their disappearance is rather mysterious in some instances, for they are certainly not all killed off. The black bear is much more easily killed, yet the black bear holds its own in many parts of the land from which the wolf has vanished. No animal is quite so difficult to kill as is the wolf, whether by poison or rifle or hound. Yet, after a comparatively few have been slain, the entire species will perhaps vanish from certain localities.

But with all wild animals it is a noticeable fact that a course of contact with man continuing over many generations of animal life causes a species so to adapt itself to its new surroundings that it ceases to diminish in numbers. When white men take up a new country, the game, and

especially the big game, being entirely
unused to contend with the new foe, suc-
cumbs easily, and is almost completely
killed out. If any individuals survive
at all, however, the succeeding generations are far more difficult to exterminate
than were their ancestors, and they cling
much more tenaciously to their old homes.

The game to be found in old and long-
settled countries is much more wary and
able to take care of itself than the game
of an untrodden wilderness. It is a very
difficult matter to kill a Swiss chamois;
but it is a very easy matter to kill a white
goat after a hunter has once penetrated
among the almost unknown peaks of the
mountains of British Columbia. When
the ranchmen first drove their cattle to
the Little Missouri they found the deer
tame and easy to kill, but the deer of
Maine and the Adirondacks test to the full
the highest skill of the hunter.

56

The Timber-wolf

In consequence, after a time, game may even increase in certain districts where settlements are thin. This has been true of the wolves throughout the northern cattle country in Montana, Wyoming, and the western ends of the Dakotas. In the old days wolves were very plentiful throughout this region, closely following the huge herds of buffaloes. The white men who followed these herds as professional buffalo-hunters were often accompanied by other men, known as "wolfers," who poisoned these wolves for the sake of their furs. With the disappearance of the buffalo the wolves seemed so to diminish in numbers that they also seemed to disappear. During the last ten years their numbers have steadily increased, and now they seem to be as numerous as they ever were in the region in question, and they are infinitely more wary and more difficult to kill.

Good Hunting

Along the Little Missouri their ravages were so serious from 1893 to 1897 as to cause heavy damage to the stockmen. Not only colts and calves, but young trail stock, and in midwinter even full-grown horses and steers, are continually slain; and in some seasons their losses have been so serious as to more than eat up all the profits of the ranchman. The county authorities put a bounty on wolf scalps of three dollars each, and in my own neighborhood the ranchmen of their own accord put on a further bounty of five dollars. This made eight dollars for every wolf, and as the skin is also worth something, the business of killing wolves was quite profitable.

Wolves are very shy, and show extraordinary cunning both in hiding themselves and in slinking out of the way of the hunter. They are rarely killed with the rifle. I have never shot but one

58

myself. They are occasionally trapped, but after a very few have been procured in this way the survivors become so wary that it is almost impossible even for a master of the art to do much with them, while an ordinary man can never get one into a trap except by accidcnt.

More can be done with poison, but even in this case the animal speedily learns caution by experience. When poison is first used in a district wolves are very easily killed, and perhaps almost all of them will be slain, but nowadays it is difficult to catch any but young ones in this way. Occasionally an old one will succumb, but there are always some who cannot be persuaded to touch a bait. The old she-wolves teach their cubs, as soon as they are able to walk, to avoid man's trace in every way, and to look out for traps and poison.

In consequence, though most cow-

59

Good Hunting

punchers carry poison with them, and are continually laying out baits, and though some men devote most of their time to poisoning for the sake of the bounty and the fur, the results are not very remunerative.

The most successful wolf-hunter on the Little Missouri in 1896 was a man who did not rely on poison at all, but on dogs. He was a hunter named Massingale, and he always had a pack of at least twenty hounds. The number varied, for a wolf at bay is a terrible fighter, with jaws like those of a steel trap and teeth that cut like knives, so that the dogs were continually disabled and sometimes killed, and the hunter had always to be on the watch to add animals to his pack.

It was not a pack that would appeal, as far as looks go, to an old huntsman, but it was thoroughly fitted for its own work. Most of the dogs were greyhounds, either rough or smooth haired, but many of them were big mongrels, and part some other breed, such as bull-dog, mastiff, Newfoundland, blood-hound, or collie.

The only two necessary requisites were that the dogs should run fast and fight gamely; and in consequence they formed as wicked, hard-biting a crew as ever ran down and throttled a wolf. They were usually taken out ten at a time, and by their aid Massingale killed two hundred wolves in the course of the year.

Of course there was no pretence of giving the game fair play. The wolves were killed as vermin, not for sport. The greatest havoc was in the spring-time, when the she-wolves were followed to their dens, which were sometimes holes in the earth and sometimes natural caves. There were from three to nine whelps in each litter. Some of the hounds were very fast, and they could usually over-

61

Good Hunting

take a young or weak wolf; but an old wolf-dog, with a good start, unless run into at once, would surely get away if he were in running trim. Frequently, however, he was caught when he was not in running trim, for the hunter was apt to find him when he had killed a calf or taken part in dragging down a horse or steer. Under these circumstances he could not run long before the pack.

If possible, as with all such packs, the hunter himself would get up in time to end the worry by a stab of his hunting-knife; but unless he was quick he would have nothing to do, for the pack was thoroughly competent to do its own killing. Grim fighter though a great wolf-dog is, he stands no show before the onslaught of ten such dogs, agile and powerful, who rush on their antagonist in a body. They possessed great power in their jaws, and unless Massingale was

The Timber-wolf

up within two or three minutes after the wolf was taken, the dogs literally tore him to pieces, though one or more of their number might be killed or crippled in the fight.

Other hunters were striving to get together packs thoroughly organized, and the wolves may be thinned out; they were certainly altogether too plentiful. During the fall of 1896 I saw a number myself, although I was not looking for them. I frequently came upon the remains of sheep and young stock which they had killed, and once, on the top of a small plateau, I found the body of a large steer, while the torn and trodden ground showed that he had fought hard for his life before succumbing. There were apparently two wolves engaged in the work, and the cunning beasts had evidently acted in concert. While one attracted the steer's attention, the other, according to the invariable wolf habit, attacked him from behind, hamstringing him and tearing out his flanks. His body was still warm when I came up, but his murderers had slunk off, either seeing or smelling me. Their handiwork was unmistakable, however, for, unlike bears and cougars, wolves invariably attack their victim at the hind-quarters, and begin their feast on the hams or flanks if the animal is of any size.

Shooting the Prong-buck

V

SHOOTING THE PRONG-BUCK

OR a few years before 1897, when I visited my cattle range I spent most of my time out on the great plains, where almost the only game that can be found is the prong-horned antelope; and as on such trips the party depends for fresh meat upon the rifle, I have on each occasion done a certain amount of antelope-shooting.

In the old days, when antelope were far more plentiful than they are now, they could often be procured by luring them

67

Good Hunting

with a red flag—for they are very inquisitive beasts — but now they have grown wary, and must usually be either stalked, which is very difficult, owing to their extreme keenness of vision and the absence of cover on the prairies, or else must be ridden into.

With first-class greyhounds and good horses they can often be run down in fair chase; but ordinarily the rider can hope for nothing more than to get within fair shooting-range, and this only by taking advantage of their peculiarity of running straight ahead in the direction in which they are pointed when once they have settled to their pace. Usually antelope, as soon as they see a hunter, run straight away from him; but sometimes they make their flight at an angle, and as they do not like to change their course when once started, it is occasionally possible to cut them off from the point towards which they are headed, and get a reasonably close shot.

In the fall of 1896 I spent a fortnight on the range with the ranch wagon. I was using for the first time one of the then new small-caliber, smokeless-powder rifles, a 30-30-160 Winchester. I had a half-jacketed bullet, the butt being cased in hard metal, while the nose was of pure lead.

While travelling to and fro across the range we usually broke camp each day, not putting up the tent at all during the trip; but at one spot we spent three nights. It was in a creek bottom, bounded on either side by rows of grassy hills, beyond which stretched the rolling prairie. The creek bed, which at this season was of course dry in most places, wound in S-shaped curves, with here and there a pool and here and there a fringe of stunted, wind-beaten timber. We were camped

69

Good Hunting

near a little grove of ash, box-alder, and willow, which gave us shade at noonday; and there were two or three pools of good water in the creek bed—one so deep that I made it my swimming-bath.

The first day that I was able to make a hunt I rode out with my foreman, Sylvane Ferris. I was mounted on Muley. Twelve years before, when Muley was my favorite cutting-pony on the round-up, he never seemed to tire or to lose his dash, but Muley was now sixteen years old, and on ordinary occasions he liked to go as soberly as possible; yet the good old pony still had the fire latent in his blood, and at the sight of game—or, indeed, of cattle or horses—he seemed to regain for the time being all the headlong courage of his vigorous and supple youth.

On the morning in question it was two or three hours before Sylvane and I saw

Shooting the Prong-buck

any game. Our two ponies went steadily forward at a single foot or shack, as the cow-punchers term what Easterners call "a fox trot." Most of the time we were passing over immense grassy flats, where the mats of short curled blades lay brown and parched under the bright sunlight. Occasionally we came to ranges of low, barren hills, which sent off gently rounding spurs into the plain.

It was on one of these ranges that we first saw our game. As we were travelling along the divide we spied eight antelope far ahead of us. They saw us as soon as we saw them, and the chance of getting to them seemed small; but it was worth an effort, for by humoring them when they start to run, and galloping towards them at an oblique angle to their line of flight, there is always some little chance of getting a shot. Sylvane was on a light buckskin horse, and I left him on the ridge crest to occupy their time while I cantered off to one side.

The prong-horns became uneasy as I galloped off, and ran off the ridge crest in a line nearly parallel to mine. They did not go very fast, and I held Muley in, who was all on fire at the sight of the game. After crossing two or three spurs, the antelope going at half speed, they found I had come closer to them, and, turning, they ran up one of the valleys between two spurs.

Now was my chance, and, wheeling at right angles to my former course, I galloped Muley as hard as I knew how up the valley nearest and parallel to where the antelope had gone. The good old fellow ran like a quarter-horse, and when we were almost at the main ridge crest I leaped off, and ran ahead with my rifle at the ready, crouching down as I came to the sky-line? Usually on such oc-

72

Shooting the Prong-buck

casions I find that the antelope have gone
on, and merely catch a glimpse of them
half a mile distant, but on this occasion
everything went right. The band had
just reached the ridge crest about two
hundred and twenty yards from me across
the head of the valley, and I halted for a
moment to look around. They were start-
ing as I raised my rifle, but the trajectory
is very flat with these small-bore smokeless-powder weapons, and taking a coarse
front sight I fired at a young buck which
stood broadside to me. There was no
smoke, and as the band raced away I
saw him sink backward, the ball having
broken his hip.

We packed him bodily behind Sylvane
on the buckskin and continued our ride,
as there was no fresh meat in camp, and
we wished to bring in a couple of bucks if
possible. For two or three hours we saw
nothing. The unshod feet of the horses

Good Hunting

made hardly any noise on the stretches of sun-cured grass, but now and then we passed through patches of thin weeds, their dry stalks rattling curiously, making a sound like that of a rattlesnake. At last, coming over a gentle rise of ground, we spied two more antelopes, half a mile ahead of us and to our right.

Again there seemed small chance of bagging our quarry, but again fortune favored us. I at once cantered Muley ahead, not towards them, so as to pass them well on one side. After some hesitation they started, not straightaway, but at an angle to my own course. For some moments I kept at a hand-gallop, until they got thoroughly settled in their line of flight; then I touched Muley, and he went as hard as he knew how.

Immediately the two panic-stricken and foolish beasts seemed to feel that I was cutting off their line of retreat, and

Shooting the Prong-buck

raced forward at mad speed. They went much faster than I did, but I had the shorter course, and when they crossed me they were not fifty yards ahead—by which time I had come nearly a mile. Muley stopped short, like the trained cow-pony he was; I leaped off, and held well ahead of the rearmost and largest buck. At the crack of the little rifle down he went with his neck broken. In a minute or two he was packed behind me on Muley, and we bent our steps towards camp.

During the remainder of my trip we were never out of fresh meat, for I shot three other bucks — one after a smart chase on horseback, and the other two after careful stalks.

The game being both scarce and shy, I had to exercise much care, and after sighting a band I would sometimes have to wait and crawl round for two or three

75

Good Hunting

hours before they would get into a position where I had any chance of approaching. Even then they were more apt to see me and go off than I was to get near them.

Antelope are the only game that can be hunted as well at noonday as in the morning or evening, for their times for sleeping and feeding are irregular. They never seek shelter from the sun, and when they lie down for a noonday nap they are apt to choose a hollow, so as to be out of the wind; in consequence, if the band is seen at all at this time, it is easier to approach them than when they are up and feeding.

They sometimes come down to water in the middle of the day, sometimes in the morning or evening. On this trip I came across bands feeding and resting at almost every time of the day. They seemed usually to feed for a couple of hours, then

STALKING BIG GAME

rest for a couple of hours, then begin feeding again.

The last shot I got was when I was out with Joe Ferris, in whose company I had killed my first buffalo, just thirteen years before, and not very far from the spot I then was at. We had seen two or three bands that morning, and in each case, after a couple of hours of useless effort, I failed to get near enough. At last, towards mid-day, we got within range of a small band lying down in a little cup-shaped hollow in the middle of a great flat. I did not have a close shot, for they were running about one hundred and eighty yards off. The buck was rear-most, and at him I aimed; the bullet struck him in the flank, coming out of the opposite shoulder, and he fell in his next bound. As we stood over him, Joe shook his head, and said, "I guess that little 30-30 is the ace"; and I told him I guessed so too.

77

A Tame White Goat

VI

A TAME WHITE GOAT

ONE of the queerest wild beasts in North America is the so-called white goat. It is found all along the highest peaks of the Rocky Mountains from Alaska into Montana, Idaho, and Washington. Really it is not a goat at all, but a kind of mountain-antelope, whose nearest kinsfolk are certain Asiatic antelopes found in the Himalayas. It is a squat, powerfully built, and rather clumsy-looking animal, about as heavy as a good-sized deer, but not as tall. It is pure white in color, except

81

that its hoofs, horns, and muzzle are jet
black.   In winter its fleece is very long,
and at that time it wears a long beard,
which makes it look still more like a goat.
It has a very distinct hump on the
shoulders, and the head is usually carried
low.

White goats are quite as queer in their
habits as in their looks.   They delight in
cold, and, except in the northernmost
portion of their range, they keep to the
very tops of the mountains; and at mid-
day, if the sun is at all powerful, retire to
caves to rest themselves.   They have the
very curious habit of sitting up on their
haunches, in the attitude of a dog begging,
when looking about for any foe whose
presence they suspect.   They are won-
derful climbers, although they have no
liveliness or agility of movement; their
surefootedness and remarkable strength
enable them to go up or down seemingly

82

A Tame White Goat

impossible places. Their great round hoofs, with sharp-cut edges, can grip the slightest projection in the rocks, and no precipice or ice-wall has any terror for them. At times they come quite low towards the foot-hills, usually to visit some mineral lick, but generally they are found only in the very high broken ground, among stupendous crags and precipices. They are self-confident, rather stupid beasts, and as they are accustomed to look for danger only from below, it is an easy matter to approach them if once the hunter is able to get above them; but they live in such inaccessible places that their pursuit entails great labor and hardship.

Their sharp black horns are eight or ten inches long, with points like needles, and their necks are thick and muscular, so that they are dangerous enemies for any foe to handle at close quarters; and they know their capacities very well, and are

Good Hunting

confident in their prowess, often prefer-
ring to stand and fight a dog or wolf
rather than to try to run. Nevertheless,
though they are such wicked and resolute
fighters, they have not a few enemies.
The young kids are frequently carried off
by eagles, and mountain-lions, wolves,
and occasionally even wolverenes prey on
the grown animals whenever they venture
down out of their inaccessible resting-
places to prowl along the upper edges of
the timber or on the open terraces of grass
and shrubby mountain plants. If a goat
is on its guard, and can get its back to a
rock, both wolf and panther will fight
shy of facing the thrust of the dagger-like
horns; but the beasts of prey are so much
more agile and stealthy that if they can
get a goat in the open or take it by surprise, they can readily pull it down.

I have several times shot white goats
for the sake of the trophies afforded by

84

the horns and skins, but I have never gone after them much, as the work is very severe, and the flesh usually affords poor eating, being musky, as there is a big musk-pod situated between the ear and the horn. Only a few of the old-time hunters knew anything about white goats; and even nowadays there are not very many men who go into their haunts as a steady thing; but the settlers who live high up in the mountains do come across them now and then, and they occasionally have odd stories to relate about them.

One was told to me by an old fellow who had a cabin on one of the tributaries that ran into Flathead Lake. He had been off prospecting for gold in the mountains early one spring. The life of a prospector is very hard. He goes alone, and in these northern mountains he cannot take with him the donkey which

85

towards the south is his almost invariable companion and beast of burden; the
tangled forests of the northern ranges
make it necessary for him to trust only
to his own power as a pack-bearer, and
he carries merely what he takes on his
own shoulders.

The old fellow in question had been
out for a month before the snow was all
gone, and his dog, a large and rather
vicious hound, to which he was greatly
attached, accompanied him. When his
food gave out he was working his way
back towards Flathead Lake, and struck
a stream, on which he found an old
dug-out canoe, deserted the previous
fall by some other prospector or pros-
pectors. Into this he got, with his
traps and his dog, and started down-
stream.

On the morning of the second day,
while rounding a point of land, he sud-

A Tame White Goat

denly came upon two white goats, a female and a little kid, evidently but a few weeks old, standing right by the stream. As soon as they saw him they turned and galloped clumsily off towards the foot of the precipice. As he was in need of meat, he shoved ashore and ran after the fleeing animals with his rifle, while the dog galloped in front. Just before reaching the precipice the dog overtook the goats. When he was almost up, however, the mother goat turned suddenly around, while the kid stopped short behind her, and she threatened the dog with lowered head. After a second's hesitation the dog once more resumed his gallop, and flung himself full on the quarry. It was a fatal move. As he gave his last leap, the goat, bending her head down sideways, struck viciously, so that one horn slipped right up to the root into the dog's chest. The blow was mortal, and the

Good Hunting

dog barely had time to give one yelp before his life passed.

It was, however, several seconds before the goat could disengage its head from its adversary, and by that time the enraged hunter was close at hand, and with a single bullet avenged the loss of his dog. When the goat fell, however, he began to feel a little ashamed, thinking of the gallant fight she had made for herself and kid, and he did not wish to harm the latter. So he walked forward, trying to scare it away; but the little thing stood obstinately near its dead mother, and butted angrily at him as he came up. It was far too young to hurt him in any way, and he was bound not to hurt it, so he sat down beside it and smoked a pipe.

When he got up it seemed to have become used to his presence, and no longer showed any hostility. For some

A Tame White Goat

seconds he debated what to do, fearing
lest it might die if left alone; then he came
to the conclusion that it was probably
old enough to do without its mother's
milk, and would have at least a chance
for its life if left to itself. Accordingly, he
walked towards the boat; but he soon
found it was following him. He tried
to frighten it back, but it belonged to
much too stout-hearted a race to yield
to pretence, and on it came after him.
When he reached the boat, after some
hesitation he put the little thing in and
started down-stream. At first the motion
of the boat startled it, and it jumped
right out into the water. When he got
it back, it again jumped out, on to a
bowlder. On being replaced the second
time, it made no further effort to escape;
but it puzzled him now and then by suddenly standing up with its fore-feet on
the very rim of the ticklish dugout, so

89

that he had to be very careful how he balanced. Finally, however, it got used to the motion of the canoe, and it was then a very contented and amusing passenger.

The last part of the journey, after its owner abandoned the canoe, was performed with the kid slung on his back. Of course it again at first objected strenuously to this new mode of progress, but in time it became quite reconciled, and accepted the situation philosophically. When the prospector reached his cabin his difficulties were at an end. The little goat had fallen off very much in flesh; for though it would browse of its own accord around the camp at night, it was evidently too young to take to the change kindly.

Before reaching the cabin, however, it began to pick up again, and it soon became thoroughly at home amid its

90

A Tame White Goat

new surroundings. It was very familiar, not only with the prospector, but with strangers, and evidently regarded the cabin as a kind of safety spot. Though it would stray off into the surrounding woods, it never ventured farther than two or three hundred yards, and after an absence of half an hour or so at the longest, it would grow alarmed, and come back at full speed, bounding along like a wild buck through the woods, until it reached what it evidently deemed its haven of refuge.

Its favorite abode was the roof of the cabin, at one corner of which, where the projecting ends of the logs were uneven, it speedily found a kind of ladder, up which it would climb until the roof was reached. Sometimes it would promenade along the ridge, and at other times mount the chimney, which it would hastily abandon, however, when a fire was lit.

Good Hunting

The presence of a dog always resulted in immediate flight, first to the roof, and then to the chimney; and when it came inside the cabin it was fond of jumping on a big wooden shelf above the fireplace, which served as a mantel-piece.

If teased it was decidedly truculent; but its tameness and confidence, and the quickness with which it recognized any friend, made it a great favorite, not only with the prospector, but with his few neighbors. However, the little thing did not live very long. Whether it was the change of climate or something wrong with its food, when the hot weather came on it pined gradually away, and one morning it was found dead, lying on its beloved roof-tree. The prospector had grown so fond of it that, as he told me, he gave it a burial "just as if it were a Christian."

FINALLY THE GOAT GOT USED TO THE MOTION OF THE CANOE

Ranching

VII

RANCHING

THERE are in every community young men to whom life at the desk or behind the counter is utterably dreary and unattractive, and who long for some out-of-door occupation which shall, if possible, contain a spice of excitement. These young men can be divided into two classes—first, those who, if they get a chance to try the life for which they long, will speedily betray their utter inability to lead it; and, secondly, those who possess the physical capacity and the

Good Hunting

peculiar mental make-up necessary for success in an employment far out of the usual paths of civilized occupations. A great many of these young men think of ranching as a business which they might possibly take up, and what I am about to say[1] is meant as much for a warning to one class as for advice to the other.

Ranching is a rather indefinite term. In a good many parts of the West a ranch simply means a farm; but I shall not use it in this sense, since the advantages and disadvantages of a farmer's life, whether it be led in New Jersey or Iowa, have often been dwelt upon by men infinitely more competent than I am to pass judgment. Accordingly, when I speak of ranching I shall mean some form of stock-raising or sheep-farming as practised now in the wilder parts of the United States,

[1] Written in 1896.

Ranching

where there is still plenty of land which,
because of the lack of rainfall, is not very
productive for agricultural purposes.

The first thing to be remembered by
any boy or young man who wishes to go
West and start life on a cattle ranch,
horse ranch, or sheep ranch is that he
must know the business thoroughly before
he can earn any salary to speak of, still
less start out on his own accord. A
great many young fellows apparently
think that a cow-boy is born and not made,
and that in order to become one all they
have to do is to wish very hard to be one.
Now, as a matter of fact, a young fellow
trained as a book-keeper would take quite
as long to learn the trade of a cow-boy
as the average cow-boy would take to
learn the trade of book-keeper. The first
thing that the beginner anywhere in the
wilder parts of the West has to learn is
the capacity to stand monotony, fatigue,

and hardship; the next thing is to learn the nature of the country.

A young fellow from the East who has been brought up on a farm, or who has done hard manual labor as a machinist, need not go through a novitiate of manual labor in order to get accustomed to the roughness that such labor implies; but a boy just out of a high-school, or a young clerk, will have to go through just such a novitiate before he will be able to command a dollar's pay. Both alike will have to learn the nature of the country, and this can only be learned by actual experience on the ground.

Again, the beginner must remember that though there is occasional excitement and danger in a ranchman's life, it is only occasional, while the monotony of hard and regular toil is not often broken. Except in the matter of fresh air and freedom from crowding, a small

Ranching

ranchman often leads a life of as grinding
hardness as the average dweller in a New
York tenement-house. His shelter is a
small log hut, or possibly a dugout in the
side of a bank, or in summer a shabby
tent. For food he will have to depend
mainly on the bread of his own baking,
on fried fat pork, and on coffee or tea
with sugar and no milk. Of course he
will occasionally have some canned stuff
or potatoes. The furniture of the hut is
of the roughest description — a roll of
blankets for bedding, a bucket, a tin
wash-basin, and a tin mug, with perhaps
a cracked looking-glass four inches square.

He will not have much society of any
kind, and the society he does have is not
apt to be over-refined. If he is a lad of a
delicate, shrinking nature and fastidious
habits, he will find much that is uncomfortable, and will need to show no small
amount of pluck and fortitude if he is to

Good Hunting

hold his own. The work, too, is often hard and often wearisome from mere sameness. It is generally done on horseback even on a sheep ranch, and always on a cow ranch. The beginner must learn to ride with indifference all kinds of rough and dangerous horses before he will be worth his keep.

With all this before him, the beginner will speedily find out that life on a Western ranch is very far from being a mere holiday. A young man who desires to start in the life ought, if possible, to have with him a little money — just enough to keep body and soul together— until he can gain a foothold somewhere.

No specific directions can be given him as to where to start. Wyoming, most of Montana, the western edge of the Dakotas, western Texas, and some portions of the Rocky Mountain States still offer chances for a man to go into the

Ranching

ranch business. In different seasons in the different localities business may be good or bad, and it would be impossible to tell where was the best place to start.

Wherever the beginner goes, he ought to make up his mind at the outset to start by doing any kind of work he can. Let him chop wood, hoe, do any chore that will bring him in twenty-five cents. If he is once able to start by showing that he is willing to work hard and do something, he can probably get employment of some kind, although this employment will almost certainly be very ill paid and not attractive. Perhaps it will be to dig in a garden, or to help one of the men drive oxen, or to do the heavy work around camp for some party of cow-punchers or lumberers. Whatever it is, let the boy go at it with all his might, and at the same time take every opportunity to get acquainted with the kind of life which he intends ultimately to lead. If he wishes to try to ride a horse, he will have every chance, if for no other reason than that he will continually meet men whose ideas of fun are met by the spectacle of a tenderfoot on a bucking bronco.

By degrees he will learn a good deal of the ways of the life and of the country. Then he must snatch the first chance that offers itself to take a position in connection with the regular work of a ranch. He may be employed as a regular hand to help cook on the ranch wagon, or taken by a shepherd to do the hard and dirty work which the shepherd would like to put off on somebody else. When he has once got as far as this his rise is certain, if he is not afraid of labor, and keeps a lookout for the opportunities that offer. After a while he will have a horse himself, and he will be employed as a second-rate man to do the ordinary ranch work.

102

Ranching

Work on a sheep ranch is less attractive, but more profitable than on any other. A good deal of skill must be shown by the shepherd in managing his flock and in handling the sheep dogs; but ordinarily it is appallingly dreary to sit all day long in the sun, or loll about in the saddle, watching the flocks of fleecy idiots. In time of storm he must work like a demon and know exactly what to do, or his whole flock will die before his eyes, sheep being as tender as horses and cattle are tough.

With the work of a cow ranch or horse ranch there comes more excitement. Every man on such a ranch has a string of eight or ten horses for his own riding, and there is a great deal of exciting galloping and hot riding across the plains; and the work in a stampede at night, or in line-riding during the winter, or in breaking the fierce little horses to the saddle, is as exciting as it is hard and dangerous.

The wilder phases of the life, however, are steadily passing away. Almost everywhere great wire fences are being put up, and no small part of the cow-boy's duty nowadays is to ride along the line of a fence and repair it wherever broken. Moreover, at present [1896] the business of cattle or horse raising on the plains does not pay well, and, except in peculiar cases, can hardly be recommended to a boy ambitious for his future.

So much for the unattractive reality of ranch life. It would be unfair not to point out that it has a very attractive side also. If the boy is fond of open-air exercise, and willing to risk tumbles that may break an occasional bone, and to endure at need heat and cold, hunger and thirst, he will find much that is pleasant in the early mornings on the great plains,

Ranching

particularly on the rare days when he is able to take a few hours' holiday to go with his shot-gun after prairie-chickens or ducks, or, perchance, to ride out with a Winchester rifle to a locality where on one of his working days he has seen a small band of antelope standing in the open, or caught a glimpse of a deer bounding through the brush. There is little temptation to spend money, unless he is addicted to the coarsest kind of dissipation, and after a few years the young fellow ought to have some hundreds of dollars laid aside. By this time he should know all about the business and the locality, and should be able to gauge just what he can accomplish.

For a year or two perhaps he can try to run a little outfit of his own in connection with his work on a big ranch. Then he will abandon the latter and start out en-

Good Hunting

tirely on his own account. Disaster may
overtake him, as it may overtake any
business man; but if he wins success, even
though of a moderate kind, he has a
pleasant life before him, riding about over
the prairie among his own horses or cattle or sheep, occasionally taking a day
off to go after game, and, while working
hard, not having to face the mere drudg-
ery which he had to encounter as a
tyro.

The chances are very small that he will
ever gain great wealth; and when he
marries and has children of his own there
are many uncomfortable problems to face,
the chief being that of schools; but for a
young man in good health and of advent-
urous temper the life is certainly pleas-
anter than that of one cooped up in the
counting-room, and while it is not one to
be sought save by the very few who have
a natural liking for it, and a natural

Ranching

capacity to enjoy it and profit by it, still for these few people it remains one of the most attractive forms of existence in America.

THE END

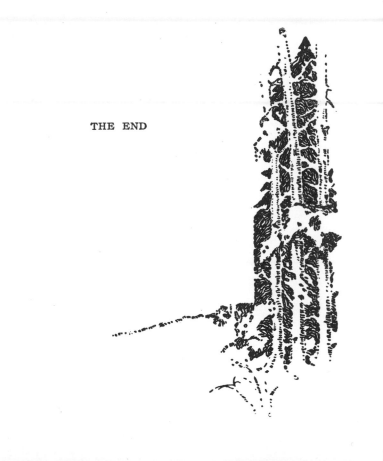